ARCHAEOPTERYX

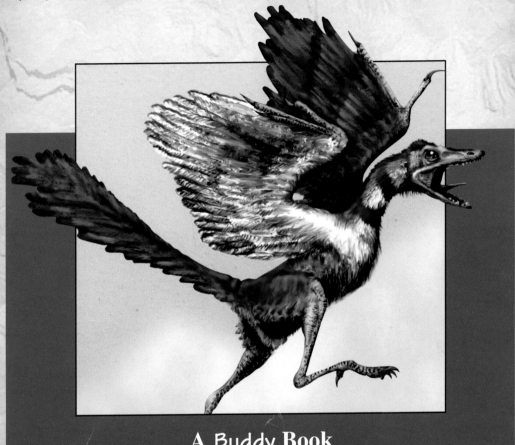

A Buddy Book
by
Richard M. Gaines

ABDO
Publishing Company

VISIT US AT
www.abdopub.com

Published by ABDO Publishing Company, 4940 Viking Drive, Edina, Minnesota 55435. Copyright © 2001 by Abdo Consulting Group, Inc. International copyrights reserved in all countries. No part of this book may be reproduced in any form without written permission from the publisher.

Published 2001
Printed in the United States of America
Second Printing 2002

Edited by: Christy De Villier
Contributing editors: Mike Goecke, Matt Ray
Graphic Design: Denise Esner, Maria Hosley
Cover Art: T. Michael Keesey, title page
Interior Photos/Illustrations: pages 4 & 15: Oil paintings by Josef Moravec; pages 5 & 20: Denise Esner; page 6: M. Shiraish ©1999 All rights reserved; page 9: Joe Tucciaroni; pages 13 & 27: Corbis; page 17: ©Douglas Henderson; page 23: Jodi Henderson; page 25; Daniel Bensen.

Library of Congress Cataloging-in-Publication Data

Gaines, Richard, 1942-
    Archaeopteryx/Richard M. Gaines.
        p. cm. – (Dinosaurs)
    Includes index.
    ISBN 1-57765-486-2
    1. Archaeopteryx—Juvenile literature. [1. Archaeopteryx. 2. Dinosaurs.] I. Title.

QE872.A8 G35 2001
562'.22—dc21

                                                                00-069985

TABLE OF CONTENTS

WHAT WERE THEY?

Archaeopteryx
Ark-ee-OP-ter-icks

The Archaeopteryx lithographica is the oldest bird-like animal we know about. Some paleontologists believe the Archaeopteryx was more like a bird than a dinosaur.

The Archaeopteryx was as big as a crow. It had giant eyes and a long tail. It did not have a beak. Instead, it had teeth inside of its long mouth.

Like birds today, the Archaeopteryx had wings. These wings had three fingers. These fingers had claws.

The Archaeopteryx's bones were thin and light. Some of these bones had air holes. These air holes made the bones light.

5

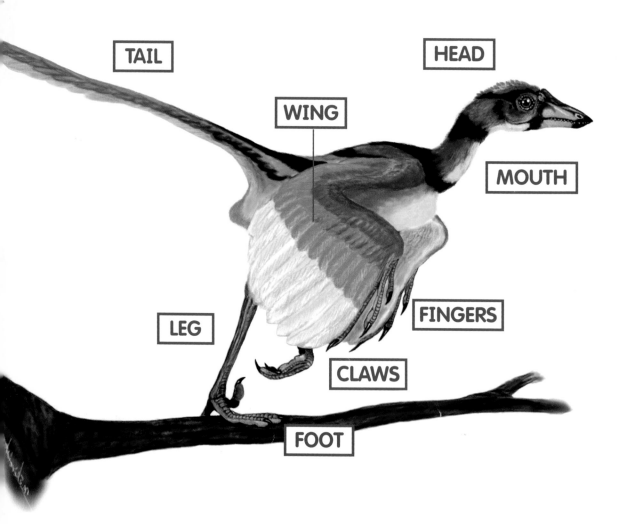

TAIL

HEAD

WING

MOUTH

LEG

FINGERS

CLAWS

FOOT

Did the Archaeopteryx fly? No, not exactly. Birds need special muscles to fly. The Archaeopteryx did not have these muscles.

Maybe the Archaeopteryx used its wings to drift in the air. How would the Archaeopteryx get off the ground? Running fast and flapping its wings would help.

The Archaeopteryx's wings were strong. Stretched out, the wings were about 18 inches (46 cm) long.

The Archaeopteryx had strong legs. It could run fast and climb trees.

The Archaeopteryx had feathers. These feathers helped this dinosaur drift through the air.

The Archaeopteryx had a special toe. This toe was like our thumb.

Look at your hand. Does your thumb face the same way as the rest of your fingers? No, it does not. Our thumbs help us hold things.

Can you find the Archaeopteryx's special toe?

The Archaeopteryx could hold onto things with its special toe. For example, it could hold onto a tree branch. This means the Archaeopteryx probably sat in trees like most birds.

WHERE DID THEY LIVE?

The Archaeopteryx lived 150 million years ago. It lived during the late Jurassic period.

The Archaeopteryx lived in Europe. A large ocean covered some of this European continent. This ocean is called the Tethys Sea. There were islands in the Tethys Sea. The Archaeopteryx lived on some of these islands.

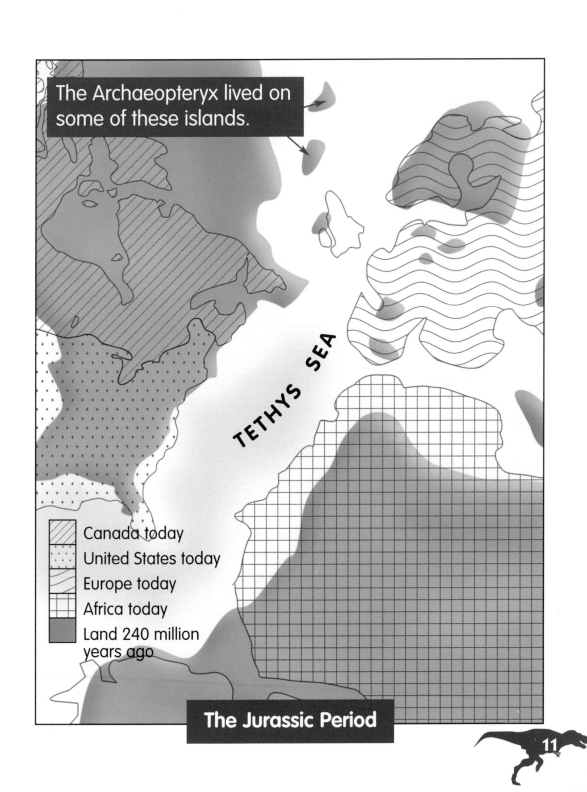

The Archaeopteryx lived on some of these islands.

TETHYS SEA

Canada today
United States today
Europe today
Africa today
Land 240 million years ago

The Jurassic Period

11

The Archaeopteryx's land was full of many low bushes. Ferns, ginkgoes, and evergreen trees, or conifers, grew there. Some of these trees grew up to 60 feet high (18 m). The Archaeopteryx could live and hide in these bushes and trees.

There were few rivers. Instead, water gathered in ponds during the rainy season. Also, pools of seawater formed near the shore.

These pools of water were the home of algae. This algae left special mud on the bottom of the pools. This mud helped to save animal and plant remains for millions of years. We call these remains fossils.

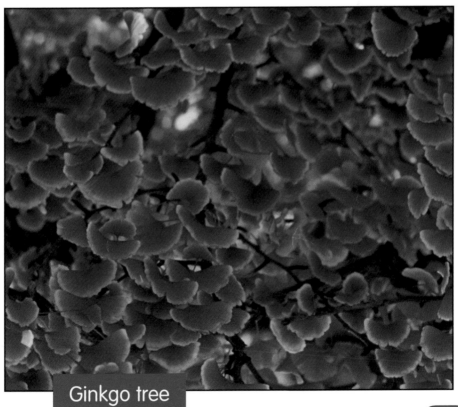

Ginkgo tree

The Archaeopteryx lived among the pterosaurs. Pterosaur means "winged lizard." These flying reptiles were not dinosaurs.

Pterosaurs flew with a special wing. The wing was made of skin, not feathers. This skin stretched from its fourth finger to the side of its body.

There was one kind of pterosaur called Rhamphorhynchus. The Rhamphorhynchus had teeth that pointed out. This pterosaur had a long tail, too.

Some pterosaurs had webbed
feet. They could swim with these
webbed feet.

Rhamphorhynchus

WHO ELSE LIVED THERE?

The Archaeopteryx lived among crocodiles, horseshoe crabs, turtles, sponges, shrimp, and jellyfish. There were lizards that looked like horned toads.

Many kinds of sharks, rays, and fish swam in the sea. Some of these early fish were up to six feet (two m) long.

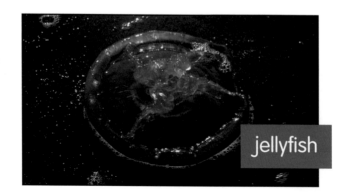

jellyfish

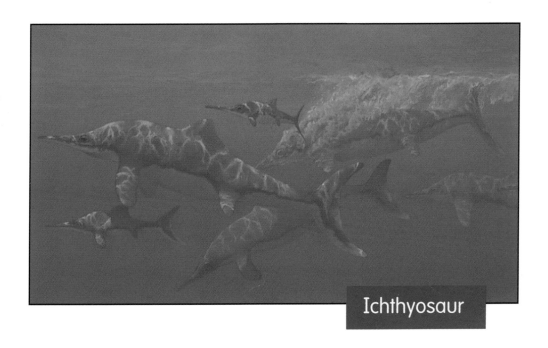

Ichthyosaur

Another neighbor of the Archaeopteryx was the Ichthyosaur. It lived in the ocean. The Ichthyosaur looked like a dolphin. It had a long nose and sharp teeth. The Ichthyosaur's arms looked like fins.

WHAT DID THEY EAT?

beetle

The Archaeopteryx ate insects.

dragonfly

The Archaeopteryx ate lizards, frogs, worms, and small snakes. Maybe this winged dinosaur caught fish.

The Archaeopteryx possibly ate any dead animals it found. This is called scavenging.

Flies, dragonflies, cockroaches, locusts, crickets, beetles, wasps, and bees were food for the Archaeopteryx. They probably swallowed these insects whole.

Compsognathus

Maybe the Compsognathus was
an enemy of the Archaeopteryx.
The Compsognathus was a small,
meat-eating dinosaur.

The Compsognathus possibly ate any Archaeopteryx it could catch. Maybe the Compsognathus tried to eat the Archaeopteryx's eggs and babies, too.

The Archaeopteryx and the Compsognathus were the same size. The bones of Compsognathus looked just like the Archaeopteryx. How did paleontologists figure out that they were two different dinosaurs? Archaeopteryx fossils show feathers. The Compsognathus did not have feathers.

21

FAMILY LIFE

Did the Archaeopteryx lay its eggs in a nest? Maybe it made a nest on the ground for the eggs. Or, perhaps the mother Archaeopteryx buried the eggs in the ground.

We do not know much about the Archaeopteryx's young. Maybe the Archaeopteryx's young were like the Gobipteryx's young. The Gobipteryx was related to the Archaeopteryx.

Eggs in a nest.

Paleontologists learned that Gobipteryx young were like today's baby chickens. Maybe these Gobipteryx chicks could fly soon after hatching. So, maybe Archaeopteryx's young could fly soon after hatching, too.

THE EARLY BIRDS

Flying birds appeared shortly after the Archaeopteryx died out. These early birds lived in Spain, Madagascar, North and South America.

The Confuciusornis was an early bird. It lived in the forests near a freshwater lake. The Confuciusornis had a beak and no teeth. This made it look like a bird of today.

Most of the early birds died out with the dinosaurs. The birds we see today are related to those early birds.

Confuciusornis

DISCOVERY

Over millions of years, the pools of water where the Archaeopteryx lived turned into limestone. Workers would cut this limestone into thin sheets for people to use.

In 1860, a limestone worker discovered a fossil in the limestone. It was a feather. Everyone knew that the feather was very old. Yet, no one knew which animal the feather belonged to.

Later, people discovered another fossil in limestone. This time, the fossil was the bones of an Archaeopteryx. This fossil also had feathers. So, people realized which animal the first feather fossil belonged to—the Archaeopteryx!

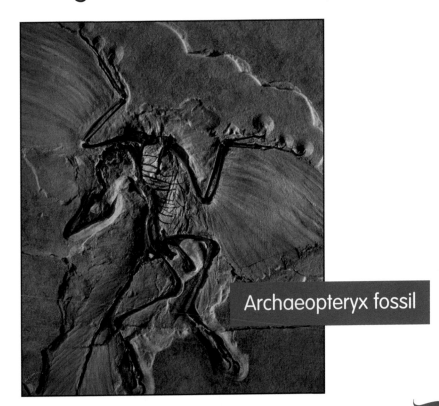

Archaeopteryx fossil

The British Museum
Great Russell Street, London, UK WC1B 3DG
www.thebritishmuseum.ac.uk

Natural History Museum of Humboldt University
Invalidenstrasse 43, D-10115 Berlin, Germany
www.museum.hu-berlin.de/start.html

Jura Museum
Burgstr. 19 D-85072 Eichstätt, Germany
www.altmuehlnet.de/hp/an01118/

Teyler Museum in Haarlem in the Netherlands
Spaarne 16, 2011 CH Haarlem, The Netherlands
www.teylersmuseum.nl/engels/hal.html

ARCHAEOPTERYX

NAME MEANS	Old wing from the printing stone
DIET	Meat, insects, fruit, seeds
WEIGHT	11-18 ounces (300-500 g)
SIZE	14 inches (36 cm)
TIME	Late Jurassic Period
FAMILY	Theropod
SPECIAL FEATURE	Feathers
FOSSILS FOUND	Germany

Archaeopteryx lived
150 million years ago

First humans appeared
1.6 million years ago

Triassic Period	Jurassic Period	Cretaceous Period	Tertiary Period
245 Million years ago	208 Million years ago	144 Million years ago	65 Million years ago
Mesozoic Era			Cenozoic Era

FUN DINOSAUR WEB SITES

Zoom Dinosaurs
www.EnchantedLearning.com/subjects/dinosaurs
Zoom Dinosaurs, designed for students of all ages, includes an illustrated dinosaur dictionary and classroom activities.

Sherlock Bones and the Case of the Disappearing Dinosaurs
www.vilenski.com/science/dinosaur/index.html
This web site explains various theories of why dinosaurs became extinct.

Dig These Dinosaurs
www.bonus.lycos.com/bonus/list/n_digthese.html
This dinosaur site has plenty of puzzles, games, and fun facts for children.

IMPORTANT WORDS

algae tiny plants that live in water, some can multiply very quickly.

conifers trees that have needles instead of leaves. Conifers stay green all year long.

continent one of the seven land masses of the earth.

dinosaur reptiles that lived on the land 248-65 million years ago.

fossil remains of very old animals and plants. People commonly find fossils in the ground.

ginkgo a tree with fan shaped leaves and yellow seeds.

Jurassic period period of time that happened 208-144 million years ago

limestone a type of rock that is made of the skeletons of tiny microorganisms.

paleontologist a scientist who studies very old life (like dinosaurs), mostly by studying fossils.

reptile an animal that breathes air, has scales, and lays eggs.

scavenge when animals eat dead animals that they did not kill themselves.

INDEX